CESAR CHAVEZ

Labor Rights Activist

Joanne Mattern

Cavendish Square

New York

Published in 2020 by Cavendish Square Publishing, LLC
243 5th Avenue, Suite 136, New York, NY 10016

Website: cavendishsq.com

This publication represents the opinions and views of the author based on his or her personal experience, knowledge, and research. The information in this book serves as a general guide only. The author and publisher have used their best efforts in preparing this book and disclaim liability rising directly or indirectly from the use and application of this book.

All websites were available and accurate when this book was sent to press.

Library of Congress Cataloging-in-Publication Data

Names: Mattern, Joanne, 1963- author.
Title: Cesar Chavez: labor rights activist / by Joanne Mattern.
Description: First edition. | New York, NY : Cavendish Square Publishing, 2020. | Series: Barrier-breaker bios | Includes bibliographical references and index. | Audience: Ages 9. | Audience: Grades 4-6.
Identifiers: LCCN 2019032217 (print) | LCCN 2019032218 (ebook) | ISBN 9781502649546 (library binding) | ISBN 9781502649522 (paperback) | ISBN 9781502649539 (set) | ISBN 9781502649553 (ebook)
Subjects: LCSH: Chavez, Cesar, 1927-1993--Juvenile literature. | United Farm Workers--History--Juvenile literature. | Labor leaders--United States--Biography--Juvenile literature. | Mexican American migrant agricultural laborers--Biography--Juvenile literature. | Migrant agricultural laborers--Labor unions--United States--History--Juvenile literature.
Classification: LCC HD6509.C48 M374 2020 (print) | LCC HD6509.C48 (ebook) | DDC 331.88/13092 [B]--dc23
LC record available at https://lccn.loc.gov/2019032217
LC ebook record available at https://lccn.loc.gov/2019032218

Editor: Alexis David
Copy Editor: Nathan Heidelberger
Associate Art Director: Alan Sliwinski
Designer: Christina Shults
Production Coordinator: Karol Szymczuk
Photo Research: J8 Media

Printed in the United States of America

TABLE OF CONTENTS

Cesar Chavez changed the world for millions of migrant workers.

CHAPTER 1

CESAR GROWS UP

Cesar Chavez wanted to make the world a better place. His work made life better for millions of farm workers.

CHEATED!

Chavez was born on March 31, 1927. He was born in Yuma, Arizona. Chavez's parents were Mexican American. They had six children. He was the second child and the first son.

Chavez's parents owned a ranch. They also owned a grocery store. A neighbor cheated the family out of both. The Chavez family had no money. They had no jobs. The family moved to California. They became **migrant workers**.

MOVING AROUND

Migrant workers pick crops. When everything is picked, migrant workers move. They move to a new place. They pick a different crop. The Chavez family moved every few months.

Chavez's parents worked in the fields every day. They picked cherries and beans in the spring. They picked corn and grapes in the summer. They picked

FAST FACT

There were no bathrooms in the fields. Migrant workers didn't have clean water to drink either.

LEARNING ON HIS OWN

Chavez didn't like school, but he did like to learn. Chavez read every book he could find. Even after he quit school and went to work, he always made time to read. Reading taught him about history. He learned about famous leaders. Knowing these things helped him succeed later in life.

cotton in the fall. They picked peas and lettuce in the winter.

QUITTING SCHOOL

Life at home was hard for Chavez. School was hard too. Chavez and other students were treated badly. They were always moving from school to school. The

Mexican migrant workers pick strawberries in this photo.

teachers knew that the students wouldn't stay at one school for long. They didn't care if the students learned.

Chavez spoke Spanish at home. At school, he had to speak English. If he didn't, he was punished. Some students bullied the students who spoke Spanish. It was hard to learn anything.

GOING TO WORK

When Chavez was fifteen, his father was in an accident. He couldn't work. Chavez quit school. He went to work in the fields to help his family.

A migrant worker and his baby are shown here outside the shack that was their home.

When Chavez was nineteen, he joined the US Navy. He was sent to a base in the Pacific Ocean. When he came home, Chavez's life began to change.

FAST FACT

Chavez attended more than thirty different schools.

Chavez protests in Chicago in 1979 for better work conditions.

CHAPTER 2

WORKING TOGETHER

When Chavez came home from the navy, he had to get a job. He also had some big ideas. Chavez wanted to help migrant workers. He wanted to make life better for all.

LOOKING FOR CHANGE

Chavez came home in 1948. Because he had so little education, he couldn't get a good job. Chavez went back to working in the fields. That same year, Chavez married Helen Fabela. She was also a migrant worker.

Chavez was tired of the way migrant workers were treated. He wanted to change things. In 1948, Chavez got some workers to go on **strike**. They wouldn't work unless they got more money. The strike only lasted a few days. The migrants lost the fight. They had to go back to work.

GET OUT IF YOU CAN

From 1951 to 1953, the Chavez family lived in a crowded **barrio**. It was called "Sal Si Puedes." That's Spanish for "get out if you can." Life in the barrio was very hard. Houses had no electricity. They had no bathrooms or running water. Some migrants lived in tents. Others lived in their cars.

THE CSO

In 1952, Chavez was picking apricots near San Jose. He met a man named Fred Ross. Ross belonged to the

Chavez is shown here with his wife, Helen Fabela.

Community Service Organization, or CSO. The CSO worked to make life better for Mexican Americans.

Chavez joined the CSO. He became a community organizer. Chavez told the workers they had to vote. If enough of them voted, things would change.

Chavez traveled around California and Arizona. He talked to workers. He started new CSO groups. In 1958, he became the director of the CSO.

HELPING FARM WORKERS

Chavez wanted to organize farm workers. Other CSO leaders said no, so Chavez took action. In 1962, he quit his job. He left the CSO.

Chavez formed his own organization. He called it the National Farm Workers Association (NFWA). Later, the name changed to the United Farm Workers (UFW). Running the UFW was hard work, but Chavez didn't mind. He knew migrants could work together. They would make big changes happen.

STRIKE!

In 1965, the UFW led grape pickers in a strike. The workers demanded better pay. They wanted better

Chavez and Fred Ross lead a march of striking farm workers.

working conditions. They refused to go back to work until things changed.

In 1966, Chavez led a 300-mile (480-kilometer) march to call attention to the grape workers' demands.

Chavez thought that the American people would support the strike. Chavez asked people to **boycott** grapes. More than seventeen million Americans did.

In 1968, Chavez went on a **hunger strike**. More people supported the workers.

VIOLENCE AND VICTORY

The grape workers stayed on strike for five long years. Finally, in 1970, the UFW won. The growers signed an agreement that made things better for the workers.

During the strike, Chavez and the workers faced violence. They were attacked. They were beaten. Through it all, Chavez told the workers that nonviolence was the answer. He didn't fight back. He told everyone to work for peace.

Later in life, Chavez spoke out about dangerous pesticides.

Chavez, on a hunger strike, appears with Robert F. Kennedy.

Chavez showed respect for others. Chavez wanted everyone to respect each other. This idea made him popular with many Americans.

FAST FACT

In 1970, Chavez and the UFW led a strike against lettuce growers.

LEARNING HOW TO ORGANIZE

Chavez was very good at organizing people. He learned this skill from his own life. He understood how hard life was for migrants. He also learned by working for local organizations. His work with the CSO taught him how to speak to others. It showed him what people cared about. It showed him that he could create change.

Chavez is shown here at the Democratic National Convention in 1976.

Chavez speaks to an interviewer shortly before his death in 1993.

CHAPTER 3

CHANGING THE WORLD

havez worked hard to make things better for farm workers. His work had many great effects.

A STRONG UNION

The National Farm Workers Association was something new. Before, there was no **union** for farm workers. Farm owners could treat workers any way they wanted. If the workers complained, they could lose their jobs.

Creating a union gave the farm workers power. They worked as a large group. Before, a few workers

Striking grape pickers marched through this vineyard in 1966.

might complain, but nothing would happen. If they went on strike, the owner would replace them. But what if thousands of workers went on strike? It was very hard for the owners to get their crops picked. The owners lost money. They had to listen to the farm workers.

FAST FACT

Cesar Chavez Day is celebrated every March 31.

MAKING A DIFFERENCE

Chavez's work taught people about migrant workers and the poor conditions they faced. Americans enjoyed eating fruits and vegetables. However, they didn't think about the people who picked those foods. Chavez's work changed that.

Thanks to Chavez, millions of people began supporting migrant workers. They demanded that workers be treated better. The farm owners had to listen.

Chavez also showed people that anyone could make a difference. Workers could demand more rights. Other people could help. They could start a boycott.

If a few people stop buying a product, nothing changes. However, when a huge group of people

Chavez won support from people all over America.

boycott the product, change happens. People can work together to change things.

Today, there are more than two million farm workers in the United States. These workers still face

FAST FACT

Chavez was awarded the Presidential Medal of Freedom in 1994.

a difficult life. Their jobs are hard and dangerous. The workers don't get paid a lot of money. However, their lives are better because of Cesar Chavez. Chavez gave workers respect. He gave them a voice.

A POWERFUL EXAMPLE

Chavez died on April 23, 1993. He was sixty-six years old. People all over the world honored him. About fifty thousand people came to his funeral.

Chavez led by example. He studied the work of Dr. Martin Luther King Jr. He saw that Dr. King was not violent. He created change in peaceful ways.

Chavez used this idea of nonviolence in his own efforts. People liked that. His popularity helped him succeed.

DOLORES HUERTA

Chavez wasn't alone in his work. He worked with another leader. Her name was Dolores Huerta. Huerta was born in 1930. Like Chavez, she faced **discrimination**. Huerta was a teacher. She knew many farm children came to school hungry. She worked with Chavez to create the NFWA. Later, she was vice president of the UFW. Huerta also led several grape boycotts. She was honored with the Eleanor Roosevelt Human Rights Award. She also received the Presidential Medal of Freedom.

Chavez's friend Dolores Huerta (*front*) carried on his dream.

Chavez fought so that everyone could be treated equally. He broke barriers and made life better for many people.

TIMELINE

1927 Cesar Chavez is born on March 31.

1942 Chavez quits school to go to work.

1952 Chavez meets Fred Ross and becomes a community organizer.

1962 Chavez forms the National Farm Workers Association (later the United Farm Workers).

1965 The UFW leads a strike against grape growers.

1968 Chavez asks Americans to boycott grapes.

1975 California passes the first law to protect the rights of farm laborers.

1993 Chavez dies on April 23.

GLOSSARY

barrio A poor, crowded area of a city where Spanish-speaking people live.

boycott To refuse to buy something as a protest.

discrimination The unfair treatment of a person because of race or another trait.

hunger strike A protest in which someone refuses to eat until demands are met.

migrant workers Workers who travel from place to place to pick crops.

strike To refuse to work in order to achieve the goal of improving conditions.

union An organized group of workers.

FIND OUT MORE

BOOKS

Gregory, Josh. *Cesar Chavez*. New York, NY:
Children's Press, 2015.

Rau, Dana Meachen. *Who Was Cesar Chavez?*
New York, NY: Grosset & Dunlap, 2017.

WEBSITE

Ducksters Education Site: Cesar Chavez

https://bit.ly/2KGBWOA

VIDEO

Cesar Chavez Biography for Kids

https://www.youtube.com/watch?v=WqmOqQe-_8U

INDEX

Page numbers in **boldface** refer to images. Entries in **boldface** are glossary terms.

ABOUT THE AUTHOR

Joanne Mattern has written many books for young readers. She especially enjoys writing biographies and learning about the lives of famous people. Mattern has also written about nature, history, sports, world cultures and countries, and many other topics. She lives in New York State with her husband, four children, and several pets.